The

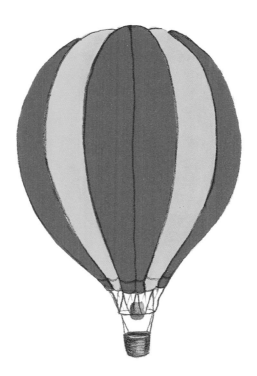

Illustrated by Trish Bowles

The red balloon
is going down.

The blue balloon
is going down.

The green balloon
is going down.

The yellow balloon
is going down.

The pink balloon
is going down.

The purple balloon
is going down.

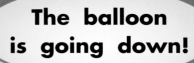

The balloon is going down!

down

going

is

going

see

the

come